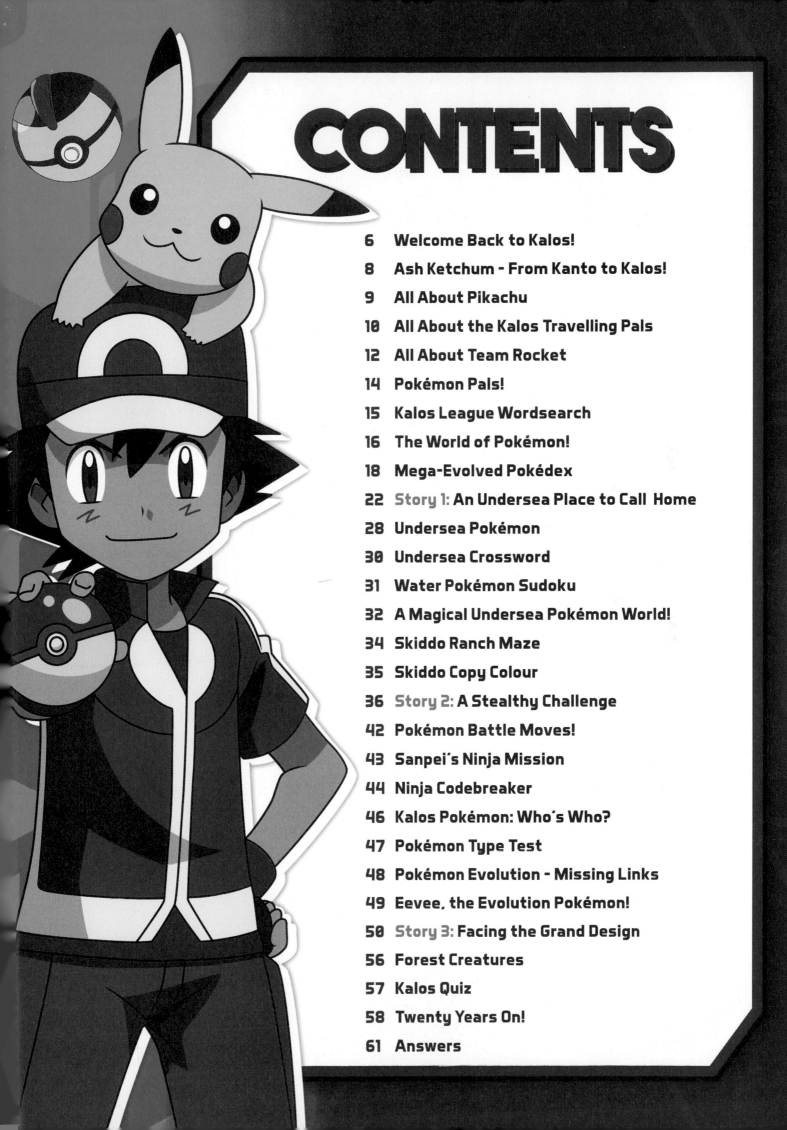

CONTENTS

THE ADVENTURE CONTINUES... WELCOME BACK TO KALOS

Ash Ketchum, Pikachu and their travelling Pokémon pals are still journeying through the vast Kalos region, with its varied and amazing landscapes, as Ash pursues his dream of becoming a Pokémon Master. The friends have had many exciting adventures, visited lots of interesting cities and places and collected some new Pokémon on their Kalos journey so far.

Ash has already won 3 Kalos Gym Badges; he needs another 5 to enter the League Championship before he can take on the ultimate battle to try and win the Kalos League. With his best pal, Pikachu, by his side, Ash is more determined than ever to succeed in his mission. He is ready to get into those battle arenas!

First stop, Coumarine city and Ash's fourth Gym battle challenge...

KALOS FIRST PARTNER POKÉMON

Each Trainer must choose from one of these three Pokémon – Chespin, Fennekin or Froakie – to start their Kalos Pokémon journey.

FROAKIE

CHESPIN

FENNEKIN

Ash, Serena, Clemont and Bonnie learn more about Pokémon Evolution and Mega-Evolved Pokémon as they visit the different regions of Kalos. They capture new Pokémon and see some of their own Pokémon evolve! What more has the incredible Kalos region got to offer the Pokémon pals? Super Pokémon Battle shows, Pokémon Spectaculars, Skiddo races, underwater exploration, ninja battles and awesome Gym battles... turn the page, there's no time to waste and plenty new Pokémon to meet!

ASH KETCHUM

FROM KANTO TO KALOS!

Ash has already learned so much from his experiences in Kalos, and his skills and Pokémon knowledge have increased, along with his own confidence in his new-found abilities. He has come a long way since the start of his Pokémon Trainer adventures in his homeland, Kanto. Of course it helps always having the support of his best pal, Pikachu, and his loyal Kalos travelling companions, Serena, Clemont and Bonnie.

His goal is to earn 5 more Kalos Gym Badges so that he can compete for the championship in the Kalos League, but he's still got time to have some fun with his friends and enjoy the awe-inspiring landscapes of Kalos.

FROAKIE
Bubble Frog Pokémon

REGION: Kalos Central
TYPE: Water
HEIGHT: 0.3m
WEIGHT: 7.0kg

The foamy bubbles that cover Froakie's body protect its sensitive skin from damage. Froakie chooses Ash as its Trainer when he first arrives in Kalos, and it becomes his Kalos First Partner Pokémon.

FROGADIER
Bubble Frog Pokémon

REGION: Kalos Central
TYPE: Water
HEIGHT: 0.6m
WEIGHT: 10.9kg

Frogadier is the first Evolution of Froakie. Ash's Froakie evolves on the second part of his Kalos journey. Frogadier coats pebbles in a bubbly foam and then flings them with pinpoint accuracy. It has spectacular jumping and climbing skills.

FLETCHLING
Tiny Robin Pokémon

REGION: Kalos Central
TYPE: Normal-Flying
HEIGHT: 0.3m
WEIGHT: 1.7kg

Flocks of Fletchling sing to each other in beautiful voices to communicate. If an intruder threatens their territory, they will defend it fiercely. Fletchling was the first Pokémon that Ash caught in Kalos.

FLETCHINDER
Ember Pokémon

REGION: Kalos Central
TYPE: Fire-Flying
HEIGHT: 0.7m
WEIGHT: 16.0kg

As the flame sac on Fletchinder's belly slowly heats up, it flies faster and faster. It produces embers from its beak. Fletchinder is the first Evolution of Fletchling.

ALL ABOUT PIKACHU

Ash and Pikachu didn't always see eye-to-eye! When he became a new Trainer, Ash was given Pikachu. He was meant to choose his First Partner Pokémon from either Charmander, Squirtle or Bulbasaur, but he overslept on the day, and Professor Oak, the leading Pokémon researcher in Kanto, gave him Pikachu instead. At first Pikachu ignored Ash and refused to travel in the usual Poké Ball method of transport. However, when Ash defended Pikachu in an attack from a flock of wild Spearow, their relationship changed and they became firm friends. Now they are inseparable and best pals! They would do anything to protect each other.

Pikachu is a rare and highly coveted Pokémon, so Ash has to protect him from attack and kidnapping attempts, especially from the terrible threesome, Team Rocket!

PIKACHU
Mouse Pokémon

REGION: Kanto

TYPE: Electric

HEIGHT: 0.4m

WEIGHT: 6.0kg

When threatened, Pikachu can deliver a powerful zap from the electric pouches on its cheeks. Its jagged tail sometimes attracts lightning during a storm.

EVOLUTION:

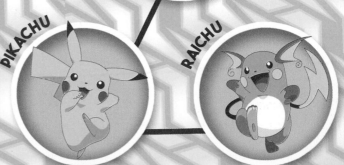

PICHU

PIKACHU

RAICHU

ALL ABOUT THE KALOS TRAVELLING PALS

SERENA

Serena's mother is a world famous Rhyhorn racer, and would love her daughter to follow in her footsteps. Serena, however, has other plans. Since joining up with Ash, Clemont and Bonnie in Kalos, she has become a young Pokémon Trainer herself and is enjoying travelling with her new friends.

When she learns about Pokémon Spectacular training, Serena decides that she wants to enter a Pokémon showcase and do a dance-battle move performance with her First Partner Pokémon, Fennekin, and her newest Pokémon, the cute Pancham.

FENNEKIN
Fox Pokémon

REGION: Kalos Central

TYPE: Fire

HEIGHT: 0.4m

WEIGHT: 9.4kg

Searing heat radiates from Fennekin's large ears to keep opponents at a distance. It often snacks on twigs to gain energy. Fennekin is Serena's First Partner Pokémon.

PANCHAM
Playful Pokémon

REGION: Kalos Central

TYPE: Fighting

HEIGHT: 0.6m

WEIGHT: 8.0kg

Pancham tries to be intimidating, but it's just too cute. When someone pats it on the head, it drops the tough-guy act and grins. It is always eager to perform – a perfect match for Serena!

BUNNELBY
Digging Pokémon

REGION: Kalos Central

TYPE: Normal

HEIGHT: 0.4m

WEIGHT: 5.0kg

Bunnelby can use its ears like shovels to dig holes in the ground. Eventually, its ears become strong enough to cut through thick tree roots while it digs. Bunnelby is Clemont's trusty go-to Pokémon for battling.

CHESPIN

Spiny Nut Pokémon

REGION: Kalos Central

TYPE: Grass

HEIGHT: 0.4m

WEIGHT: 9.0kg

When Chespin flexes its soft quills, they become tough spikes with sharp, piercing points. It relies on its nutlike shell for protection in battle. Chespin is Clemont's First Partner Pokémon.

BONNIE

Bonnie is Clemont's demanding and impulsive younger sister. She adores her big brother and is constantly trying to find a girlfriend to look after him! She is too young to have her own Pokémon, but she helps Clemont care for his Pokémon. She is particularly fond of Dedenne, and can't wait to be old enough to take charge.

LUXIO

Spark Pokémon

REGION: Sinnoh

TYPE: Electric

HEIGHT: 0.9m

WEIGHT: 30.5kg

Luxio can cause its attackers to faint by blasting them with high-voltage electricity from its sharp claws. The slightest scratch can knock an opponent out cold! Luxio live in small groups. Luxio is one of Clemont's oldest Pokémon — they first met when Clemont was still a student.

CLEMONT

Clemont is a Pokémon Trainer and the Luminose Gym Leader. This shy, reserved young man is very intelligent and is something of a genius inventor! He's actually happiest when he is working on his unusual and unique inventions and helping his friends.

Unfortunately, not all of Clemont's inventions work in quite the way he expects them to!

DEDENNE

Antenna Pokémon

REGION: Kalos Coastal

TYPE: Electric-Fairy

HEIGHT: 0.2m

WEIGHT: 2.2kg

Dedenne uses its whiskers like antennas to communicate over long distances using electrical waves. It can soak up electricity through its tail. Clemont is keeping Dedenne for his sister until she is old enough to become a Pokémon Trainer herself.

ALL ABOUT TEAM ROCKET

Wherever there's trouble, then this terrible threesome is usually to be found nearby! Team Rocket – Jessie, James and Meowth – mean-spirited villains, always ready to cause mischief and mayhem. They work for a criminal organisation run by the elusive and evil crime lord, Giovanni. Their mission is to steal valuable Pokémon, and they would love to get their dirty hands on Pikachu.

Luckily for Ash and his friends, Team Rocket's villainous plans usually fail spectacularly! However ridiculous their schemes, you have to give them 10 out of 10 for effort – Team Rocket never give up!

JESSIE

Vain, self-deluded and sharp-tongued, the purple-haired Jessie is the self-appointed leader of the Team. She hates weakness in others and would never let her teammates know that she needs them. Her short temper and argumentative nature keep them at arm's length. Jessie would rather keep up her 'tough' image then ever reveal her real feelings and emotions.

JAMES

This floppy-haired boy left his wealthy family to join the criminal world. He may love his own Pokémon, but don't be fooled – James has a nasty side to his nature. He is mean and sly, and doesn't have any qualms about stealing Pokémon to make a few quid for himself!

INKAY

Revolving Pokémon

REGION: Kalos Coastal

TYPE: Dark-Psychic

HEIGHT: 0.4m

WEIGHT: 3.5kg

The spots on Inkay's body emit a flashing light. This light confuses its opponents, giving it a chance to escape. Inkay is James' Pokémon – they share a very strong bond – and it is dedicated to the villainous cause.

PUMPKABOO

Pumpkin Pokémon

REGION: Kalos Mountain

TYPE: Ghost-Grass

HEIGHT: 0.4m

WEIGHT: 5.0kg

The nocturnal Pumpkaboo tends to get restless as darkness falls. Stories say it serves as a guide for wandering spirits, leading them through the night to find their true home. Pumpkaboo is the first Pokémon that Jessie captures in the Kalos region.

MEOWTH

This self-taught, smooth-talking cat is the brains behind the Team Rocket operation, although so far, he hasn't managed to steer the other two blundering members to success with his crazy evil schemes!

WOBBUFFET

Patient Pokémon

REGION: Kalos Coastal

TYPE: Psychic

HEIGHT: 1.3m

WEIGHT: 28.5kg

Wobbuffet prefers to hide in dark places, where its black tail can't be seen, and avoids battle when possible. However, if another Pokémon attacks it first, it puffs up its body and strikes back. Wobbuffet is Jessie's Pokémon. He tries to stay in the background, but often gets unwillingly dragged into the action.

MEOWTH

Scratch Cat Pokémon

REGION: Kanto

TYPE: Normal

HEIGHT: 0.4m

WEIGHT: 4.2kg

Meowth is attracted to round and shiny objects. Being mainly nocturnal, it likes to roam the streets at night looking for and gathering any sparkly objects it finds, especially coins. It has a gold oval coin embedded in its forehead. Team Rocket's Meowth is unique because he can speak the human language and walk on two legs instead of four.

POKÉMON PALS!

Ash, Serena, Clemont and Bonnie are looking forward to continuing their travels through Kalos together. What will their next adventure be? Grab your pens and pencils and colour this awesome foursome and their Pokémon!

KALOS LEAGUE WORDSEARCH

Ash has already earned 3 of the 8 Gym Badges he needs to enter the League Championship.

Find the names of all 8 Kalos Gym Leaders, the 8 cities the gyms are located in, in the grid below.

Remember the words could be running in any direction – vertically, horizontally, diagonally or back-to-front. If you really want to challenge yourself, try matching each Gym Leader to the city their Gym is in!

```
B O O Z L G E C Q E T V W C R
G D P B P Q S I G B E R D J N
W I F B L Y M O A M T H T E S
Y S H A L O U R Y I Z R G N X
R I G T N E K G W U L F R I C
J M C E G A L L Y C Z Z A R S
J G M R O U T L U W I Y N A X
Q A R H I B H I E X Q D T M S
H R A J L F Z L C B B P J U N
H U M L H V K E J O W A L O Q
A C O H V Z A L V L Q O A C L
U N S Q G E Z B S Y T B N K M
O T I J P M N D Y M N K I S J
E N U R N U V U Q P L X S G R
T Q E R R E V A L I I U T I D
S C L E M O N T L A W L A D R
A L O I V W K A Y E T L R F V
S J S J K U R U H K R N C K A
W I H S R R N M J Y D I A Y D
U Q E S O N I M U L G W E S A
```

- [ ] VIOLA
- [ ] GRANT
- [ ] KORRINA
- [ ] RAMOS
- [ ] CLEMONT
- [ ] VALERIE
- [ ] OLYMPIA
- [ ] WULFRIC
- [ ] ANISTAR
- [ ] COUMARINE
- [ ] SANTALUNE
- [ ] LAVERRE
- [ ] SNOWBELLE
- [ ] SHALOUR
- [ ] CYLLAGE
- [ ] LUMINOSE

THE WORLD OF Pokémon!

As all Pokémon Trainers know, the best way to win battles and to care for their Pokémon is to stay ahead of the game with an expert knowledge of the facts and stats about all the Pokémon species. Armed with a Pokédex to help them brush up on their knowledge of species, types, moves and evolutions, Trainers, novice or expert, can master almost any Pokémon challenge that comes their way!

There are 18 types of Pokémon based on their special characteristics, and all Pokémon belong to a specific species. Some Pokémon are dual-types. Knowing the types and species of Pokémon allows Trainers and Masters alike to understand a Pokémon's strengths and weaknesses and how these can be best used in battle.

The 18 types of Pokémon are:

BUNNELBY

NORMAL

FENNEKIN

FIRE

FROAKIE

WATER

CHESPIN

GRASS

PIKACHU

ELECTRIC

MIENFOO

FIGHTING

CUBCHOO

ICE

STUNKY

POISON

GOLETT

GROUND

NOIVERN

FLYING

GEODUDE

ROCK

MIME JR.

PSYCHIC

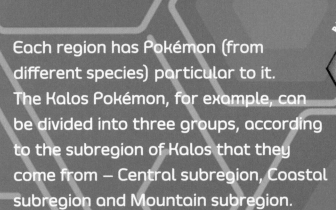
LEDYBA

BUG

HONEDGE

STEEL

UMBREON

DARK

SALAMENCE

DRAGON

Each region has Pokémon (from different species) particular to it. The Kalos Pokémon, for example, can be divided into three groups, according to the subregion of Kalos that they come from — Central subregion, Coastal subregion and Mountain subregion.

BANETTE

GHOST

SPRITZEE

FAIRY

Some Pokémon evolve into different Pokémon. Go to page 18 to learn all about the awesome Mega-Evolved Pokémon! There are also two groups of special Pokémon — Legendary and Mythical. These Pokémon are more powerful and more difficult to catch.

Kalos Legendary Pokémon

XERNEAS

ZYGARDE

YVELTAL

Kalos Mythical Pokémon

DIANCIE

HOOPA

Mega-Evolved Pokédex

When Ash first started travelling in Kalos, he learned about a new kind of Pokémon Evolution. Fully evolved Pokémon can reach a higher level of power – Mega-Evolved – but only during a battle. Once the battle is over, the Mega-Evolved Pokémon returns to its normal state. Some Mega-Evolved Pokémon have different stats from their normal pre-battle form.

Check out these awesome battle creatures! There are 39 so far.

MEGA ABOMASNOW
Frost Tree Pokémon
TYPE: Grass-Ice
HEIGHT: 2.7m
WEIGHT: 185.0kg

MEGA ABSOL
Disaster Pokémon
TYPE: Dark
HEIGHT: 1.2m
WEIGHT: 49.0kg

MEGA ALTARIA
Humming Pokémon
TYPE: Dragon-Flying
HEIGHT: 1.09m
WEIGHT: 20.6kg

MEGA AERODACTYL
Fossil Pokémon
TYPE: Rock-Flying
HEIGHT: 2.1m
WEIGHT: 79.0kg

MEGA AGGRON
Iron Armour Pokémon
TYPE: Steel
HEIGHT: 2.2m
WEIGHT: 395.0kg

MEGA AUDINO
Hearing Pokémon
TYPE: Normal-Fairy
HEIGHT: 1.50m
WEIGHT: 32.0kg

MEGA ALAKAZAM
Psi Pokémon

TYPE: Psychic

HEIGHT: 1.2m

WEIGHT: 48.0kg

MEGA AMPHAROS
Light Pokémon

TYPE: Electric-Dragon

HEIGHT: 1.4m

WEIGHT: 61.5kg

MEGA BANETTE
Marionette Pokémon

TYPE: Ghost

HEIGHT: 1.2m

WEIGHT: 13.0kg

MEGA BLASTOISE
Shellfish Pokémon

TYPE: Water

HEIGHT: 1.6m

WEIGHT: 101.1kg

MEGA BLAZIKEN
Blaze Pokémon

TYPE: Fire-Fighting

HEIGHT: 1.9m

WEIGHT: 52.0kg

MEGA CHARIZARD X
Flame Pokémon

TYPE: Fire-Dragon

HEIGHT: 1.7m

WEIGHT: 110.5kg

MEGA CHARIZARD Y
Flame Pokémon

TYPE: Fire-Flying

HEIGHT: 1.7m

WEIGHT: 100.5kg

MEGA GARCHOMP
Mach Pokémon

TYPE: Dragon-Ground

HEIGHT: 1.9m

WEIGHT: 95.0kg

MEGA GARDEVOIR
Embrace Pokémon

TYPE: Psychic

HEIGHT: 1.6m

WEIGHT: 48.4kg

MEGA BEEDRILL
Poison Bee Pokémon

TYPE: Bug-Poison

HEIGHT: 1.40m

WEIGHT: 40.5kg

MEGA CAMERUPT
Eruption Pokémon

TYPE: Fire-Ground

HEIGHT: 2.49m

WEIGHT: 320.5kg

MEGA DIANCIE
Jewel Pokémon

TYPE: Rock-Fairy

HEIGHT: 1.09m

WEIGHT: 27.8kg

MEGA GENGAR
Shadow Pokémon

TYPE: Ghost-Poison

HEIGHT: 1.4m

WEIGHT: 40.5kg

MEGA GYARADOS
Atrocious Pokémon

TYPE: Water-Dark

HEIGHT: 6.5m

WEIGHT: 305.0kg

MEGA HERACROSS
Single Horn Pokémon

TYPE: Bug-Fighting

HEIGHT: 1.7m

WEIGHT: 62.5kg

MEGA HOUNDOOM
Dark Pokémon

TYPE: Dark-Fire

HEIGHT: 1.9m

WEIGHT: 49.5kg

MEGA KANGASKHAN
Parent Pokémon

TYPE: Normal

HEIGHT: 2.2m

WEIGHT: 100.0kg

MEGA LUCARIO
Aura Pokémon

TYPE: Fighting-Steel

HEIGHT: 1.3m

WEIGHT: 57.5kg

MEGA MANECTRIC
Discharge Pokémon

TYPE: Electric

HEIGHT: 1.8m

WEIGHT: 44.0kg

MEGA MAWILE
Deceiver Pokémon

TYPE: Steel-Fairy

HEIGHT: 1.0m

WEIGHT: 23.5kg

MEGA MEDICHAM
Meditate Pokémon

TYPE: Fighting-Psychic

HEIGHT: 1.3m

WEIGHT: 31.5kg

MEGA GALLADE
Blade Pokémon

TYPE: Psychic-Fighting

HEIGHT: 1.60m

WEIGHT: 56.4kg

MEGA GLALIE
Face Pokémon

TYPE: Ice

HEIGHT: 2.11m

WEIGHT: 350.2kg

MEGA LATIAS
Eon Pokémon

TYPE: Dragon-Psychic

HEIGHT: 1.80m

WEIGHT: 52.0kg

MEGA MEWTWO X
Genetic Pokémon

TYPE: Psychic-Fighting

HEIGHT: 2.3m

WEIGHT: 127.0kg

MEGA MEWTWO Y
Genetic Pokémon

TYPE: Psychic

HEIGHT: 1.5m

WEIGHT: 33.0kg

MEGA PINSIR
Stag Beetle Pokémon

TYPE: Bug-Flying

HEIGHT: 1.7m

WEIGHT: 59.0kg

MEGA SCIZOR
Pincer Pokémon

TYPE: Bug-Steel

HEIGHT: 2.0m

WEIGHT: 125.0kg

MEGA TYRANITAR
Armour Pokémon

TYPE: Rock-Dark

HEIGHT: 2.5m

WEIGHT: 255.0kg

MEGA VENUSAUR
Seed Pokémon

TYPE: Grass-Poison

HEIGHT: 2.4m

WEIGHT: 155.5kg

MEGA LATIOS
Eon Pokémon

TYPE: Dragon-Psychic

HEIGHT: 2.31m

WEIGHT: 70.0kg

MEGA LOPUNNY
Rabbit Pokémon

TYPE: Normal-Fighting

HEIGHT: 1.30m

WEIGHT: 28.3kg

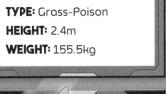

MEGA METAGROSS
Iron Leg Pokémon

TYPE: Steel-Psychic

HEIGHT: 2.49m

WEIGHT: 942.9kg

STORY: AN UNDERSEA PLACE TO CALL HOME

Ash and his travelling pals are on their way to Cyllage City for Ash's fourth Kalos Gym battle against Gym Leader Grant. They stop at a beach on the Muraille Coast for a break and lunch, before they do more battle training.

"As we're at the beach, let's have a little fun with this fishing rod!" said Serena. "Cool! And maybe you'll catch a really cute Pokémon!" cried Bonnie, excitedly. "Yeah, if you catch another Water type Pokémon, like your Froakie, you'll probably have a much easier time when you battle with Grant," said Clemont. "He uses Rock types."
"What a great idea!" cried Ash. "Can't wait to see what we catch!"

"Wow! I've got something!" laughed Ash a few minutes later, struggling to hold the rod. "Man, this thing is strong!"
"Oh goody! What could it be?" said Bonnie. "Maybe it's a Corsola or a Wailord?"
The friends gathered around Ash.
"Oh, too bad. It's just a bunch of kelp," sighed Serena.
"No guys!" shouted Clemont. "It's a Pokémon. It's a Skrelp!"
"I've never seen a Skrelp before," said Ash. "It doesn't look too happy to see us." The Skrelp suddenly leapt out of Ash's hands and bit Pikachu really hard.

"Pikachu's hurt," shouted Clemont.
"Quick, we need to get help right away!"
Ash gently picked up Pikachu.
"Don't worry, my friend," he whispered.
"You're going to be OK."
As the friends left the beach, a van pulled
up alongside them.
"Hi, my name's Eddy and this is my wife,
Lindsey," said the driver of the van.
"Is something wrong?"
"My Pikachu has been bitten by
a Skrelp," explained Ash.
"It looks like it's been poisoned,"
said Lindsey. "Eddy, get the
antidote from the first aid kit."
Lindsey gave Pikachu the antidote.
The little Pokémon slowly
opened its eyes.
"Pikachu! You're OK!" Ash sighed with
relief. "Thank you so much!"
"Just glad to be able to help," said Eddy.
"Lindsey and I work near here. We're
underwater archeologists."

"Wow! Are you exploring these
waters?" asked Serena.
"Yes. In fact we'll be diving in this
area today," said Lindsey. "We're
trying to find the sunken ship called
the Cussler. We believe that a strong
current brought it here."
"Can we help you in any way?"
asked Serena.
"Well, it could be dangerous,"
explained Lindsey. "But I can take
two of you kids down with me in the
submarine. The rest of you can stay
with Eddy and monitor us from
our base lab."
"Ash, Serena, you go," said Clemont.
"Bonnie and I will check out the lab."

Meanwhile, trouble in the form of the terrible threesome, Team Rocket, was lurking not far away...

"That sounds very interesting!" said James. "The Cussler, the luxury liner that sank while carrying priceless treasures onboard..."

"If we can get our paws on that booty, we'll be rich beyond our wildest dreams!" chuckled Meowth.

"Let's go get it!" cried Jessie.

Onboard the submarine, Ash and Serena stared through the viewing windows in amazement.

"This is awesome!" cried Ash. "Look, Qwilfish, Octillery and Skrelp!"

Suddenly, the submarine started shaking!

"What's going on down there?" cried Eddy over the radio.

"It's the current – we're being swept along, like the Cussler," said Lindsey. "Don't worry, I've got this under control. This is great – it proves our theory about the current is correct!"

"And look – there's the Cussler!" cried Serena, excitedly.

"Those Dragalge are using their special acid to fuse the parts of the ship together to create one gigantic structure!" explained Lindsey.

"It's like a paradise home for all the Water-type Pokémon!" said Ash.

As the friends continued to watch all the Water-type Pokémon, a bright light suddenly blinked on in the darkness of the deep water.

"What's that inside the Cussler?" asked Lindsey.

"Oh no!" shouted Ash. "It's Team Rocket in their submarine."

"Team Rocket? Who are they?" asked Lindsey.

"They're the bad guys who steal other people's Pokémon!" groaned Serena.

"Let's follow them and see what they're up to," said Lindsey.

"Be careful guys!" called Eddy from the base.

"We will be," said Ash.

Inside the wreck of the Cussler, Team Rocket was searching for treasure.

"A treasure trove of riches awaits us!" cackled Meowth.

"Ouch!" cried James. "What was that?"

Dozens of Skrelp started to surround the meddling trio.

"Argh! I think they are trying to tell us to go!" cried James.

"No! This is our treasure!" screamed Jessie.

"Stop! We've caught you red-handed!" cried Ash.

"The bounty on this boat is ours to take," cried Jessie.

"And just how do you think you are going to get away with this?" asked Serena.

"Ha, ha, ha! We're going to blast this treasure safe out of the water!" laughed Meowth.

"Oh no! Quick, we've got to get out of here," shouted Lindsey. "If that explosion opens up a hole in the shipwreck, water will flood the whole area!"

As Team Rocket blasted off with the treasure, the Cussler started to fill with water.

"It's going to collapse!" cried Lindsey. "We've got to do something to keep that from happening."

Ash looked around. "I've got an idea! Froakie, go help the other Pokémon!" He called out to the Water-type Pokémon and asked them to push against the sides of the ship to stop it collapsing. They all rushed to help. "Dragalge! Use your acid to seal the hole!" Ash shouted. "Froakie, Skrelp, go after Team Rocket."

"Well done everyone! We've done it!" laughed Lindsey.

"But Team Rocket got away with the treasure," sighed Serena.

"Not for long!" laughed Ash. "I don't think they'll get very far with those giant whirlpools and Froakie on their trail!"

"Ahhh! I'm dizzy!" screamed Jessie.

"Noooo, we've dropped the safe!" groaned Meowth.

"It's time to disappear I think," cried James. "Let's blast off team!"

"Ash, where are Froakie and Skrelp?" asked Serena. "Even Water types can't withstand a whirlpool like that one!"

The giant whirlpool had spun Team Rocket sky high out of the water. Poor Froakie and Skrelp were now being dragged into its swirling current. "Jump Froakie!" screamed Ash. "Take Skrelp on your back."

Ash and his friends looked on in horror. But then suddenly, Froakie and Skrelp were clear of the swirling waters. "Wow! Froakie, you were awesome!" cried Serena. "That was some jump…"

"Hey, maybe we could use that in our Gym battle against Grant…?" laughed Ash.

Ash and his friends gathered at the base lab to say goodbye to Eddy and Lindsey. "Thank you so much!" said Serena. "That was an amazing undersea adventure!"

"Our pleasure!" smiled Eddy and Lindsey. "And thank you for helping us save the Cussler and figure out which current brought the Cussler to this location."

All's well that ends well! Ash and his friends set off once again on their journey to Cyllage City Gym. And with Froakie's awesome jump moves, who knows, Ash just might earn his next badge…

Undersea Pokémon

Ash discovered some weird and wonderful new Pokémon when he went on his underwater adventure. Take a look! Which watery Pokémon is your favourite?

CHINCHOU
Angler Pokémon

REGION: Kalos Coastal

TYPE: Water-Electric

HEIGHT: 0.5m

WEIGHT: 12.0kg

Chinchou live deep in the ocean, where they flash the lights on their antennae to communicate. They can also pass electricity between their antennae.

ALOMOMOLA
Caring Pokémon

REGION: Kalos Coastal

TYPE: Water

HEIGHT: 1.2m

WEIGHT: 31.6kg

When Alomomola finds injured Pokémon in the open sea where it lives, it gently wraps its healing fins around them and guides them to shore.

HUNTAIL
Deep Sea Pokémon

REGION: Kalos Coastal

TYPE: Water

HEIGHT: 01.7m

WEIGHT: 27.0kg

Huntail lives in the depths of the ocean, where it's always dark. Its lit tail, which resembles a small creature, sometimes tricks others into attacking.

LUVDISC
Rendezvous Pokémon

REGION: Kalos Coastal

TYPE: Water

HEIGHT: 0.6m

WEIGHT: 8.7kg

During certain times of the year, so many Luvdisc gather around a single reef that the water appears to turn pink. They are rumored to bring endless love to couples who find them.

SEADRA
Dragon Pokémon

REGION: Kalos Coastal

TYPE: Water

HEIGHT: 1.2m

WEIGHT: 25.0kg

The bristling spikes that cover Seadra's body are very sharp, so touching it is not recommended. It can swim in reverse by flapping its large fins.

DRAGALGE
Mock Kelp Pokémon

REGION: Kalos Coastal

TYPE: Poison-Dragon

HEIGHT: 1.8m

WEIGHT: 81.5kg

Toxic and territorial, Dragalge defend their homes from anything that enters. Dragalge are the evolved form of Skrelp. They look very much like drifting kelp when they are swimming with the current.

REMORAID
Jet Pokémon

REGION: Kalos Coastal

TYPE: Water

HEIGHT: 0.6m

WEIGHT: 12.0kg

Remoraid is a master marksman, using sprays of water to shoot down moving targets hundreds of feet away. It often attaches itself to a Mantine in hopes of sharing a meal.

SKRELP
Mock Kelp Pokémon

REGION: Kalos Coastal

TYPE: Poison-Water

HEIGHT: 0.5m

WEIGHT: 7.3kg

Skrelp camouflages itself as rotten kelp to hide from its enemies, and while it stores up energy until it's able to evolve. It defends itself by spraying a poisonous liquid.

MAGIKARP
Fish Pokémon

REGION: Kalos Coastal

TYPE: Water

HEIGHT: 0.9m

WEIGHT: 10.0kg

Magikarp is widely regarded as the weakest Pokémon in the world. It lacks both speed and strength.

OCTILLERY
Jet Pokémon

REGION: Kalos Coastal

TYPE: Water

HEIGHT: 0.9m

WEIGHT: 28.5kg

Octillery doesn't like being out in the open. It hides itself among craggy rocks, where it can spray ink to keep enemies away without revealing itself.

STARMIE
Mysterious Pokémon

REGION: Kalos Coastal

TYPE: Water-Psychic

HEIGHT: 1.1m

WEIGHT: 80.0kg

The gem-like core at Starmie's center emits light of many colors. It is also thought to produce radio waves at night.

Undersea Crossword

Have you got what it takes to be a Pokémon Trainer? You need to be observant, quick-thinking, always alert and never give up when the going gets tough! Test out your skills and knowledge of Ash's watery undersea adventure by answering the clues below and completing this challenging crossword.

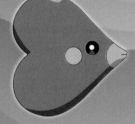

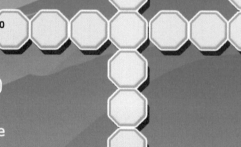

Across

3 Which underwater Pokémon disguises itself as rotten kelp? (6)

5 This Pokémon is rumoured to bring endless love to couples who find it. (7)

7 It lives in the depths of the ocean and its tail resembles a small creature Which Pokémon is it? (7)

9 Which Water-Electric type Pokémon commumicates with flashing lights on its antennae? (8)

10 The Fish Pokémon considered to be the weakest Pokémon in the world! (8)

Down

1 This Water type Pokémon is a master marksman. Who is it? (8)

2 The friends see a Water-Poison type Pokémon covered in venomous spikes, near the wreck. Its name begins with Q. Who is it? (8)

4 Name the toxic evolved Pokémon form of Skrelp. (8)

6 The name of the sunken ship that Ash, Serena and Lindsey go to view in the submarine? (7)

8 What is the name of the Kalos coast that Ash and his friends are exploring? (8)

WATER POKÉMON SUDOKU

Ash and Serena see some amazing underwater Pokémon when Lindsey takes them in her submarine to view the Cussler shipwreck. Help them work out which of these amazing watery creatures is missing from the Sudoku grid. Remember that each of the six Pokémon must only appear once on each horizontal and vertical line. Write the number of each Pokémon into the correct box on the grid.

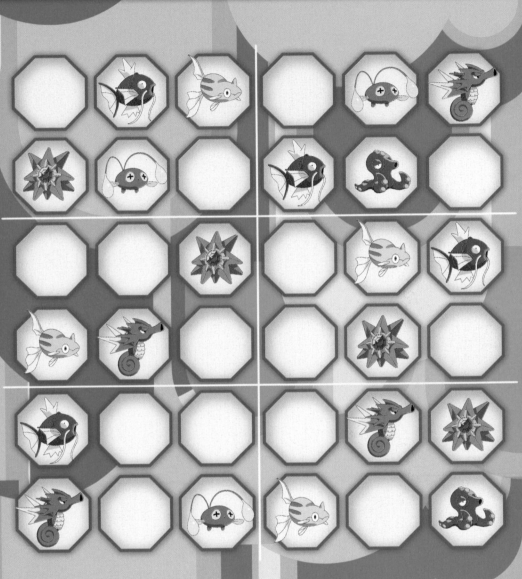

Can you name all 6 undersea Pokémon?

1 .... 4 ....

2 .... 5 ....

3 .... 6 ....

1   2   3   4   5   6

A Magical Undersea Pokémon World

Using you awesome knowledge of Water-type Pokémon and the information in this super-cool Annual, draw and colour your own undersea adventure for Ash and his friends!

Add in rocks, shells and seaplants for your Pokémon to hide behind. You could even have your own shipwreck for Ash to explore!

Grab your coloured pens and get imagining!

SKIDDO RANCH MAZE

When the Pokémon pals stop at a famous Skiddo dairy ranch on their travels, they discover Team Rocket trying to steal the ranch's delicious cheese and ice-cream, which is made from Skiddo milk. Serena races after them. Help her catch them before they make off with all the Skiddo dairy goodies!

Which two Normal-Flying type Pokémon does Serena pass as she chases after Team Rocket?

1.
....

2.
....

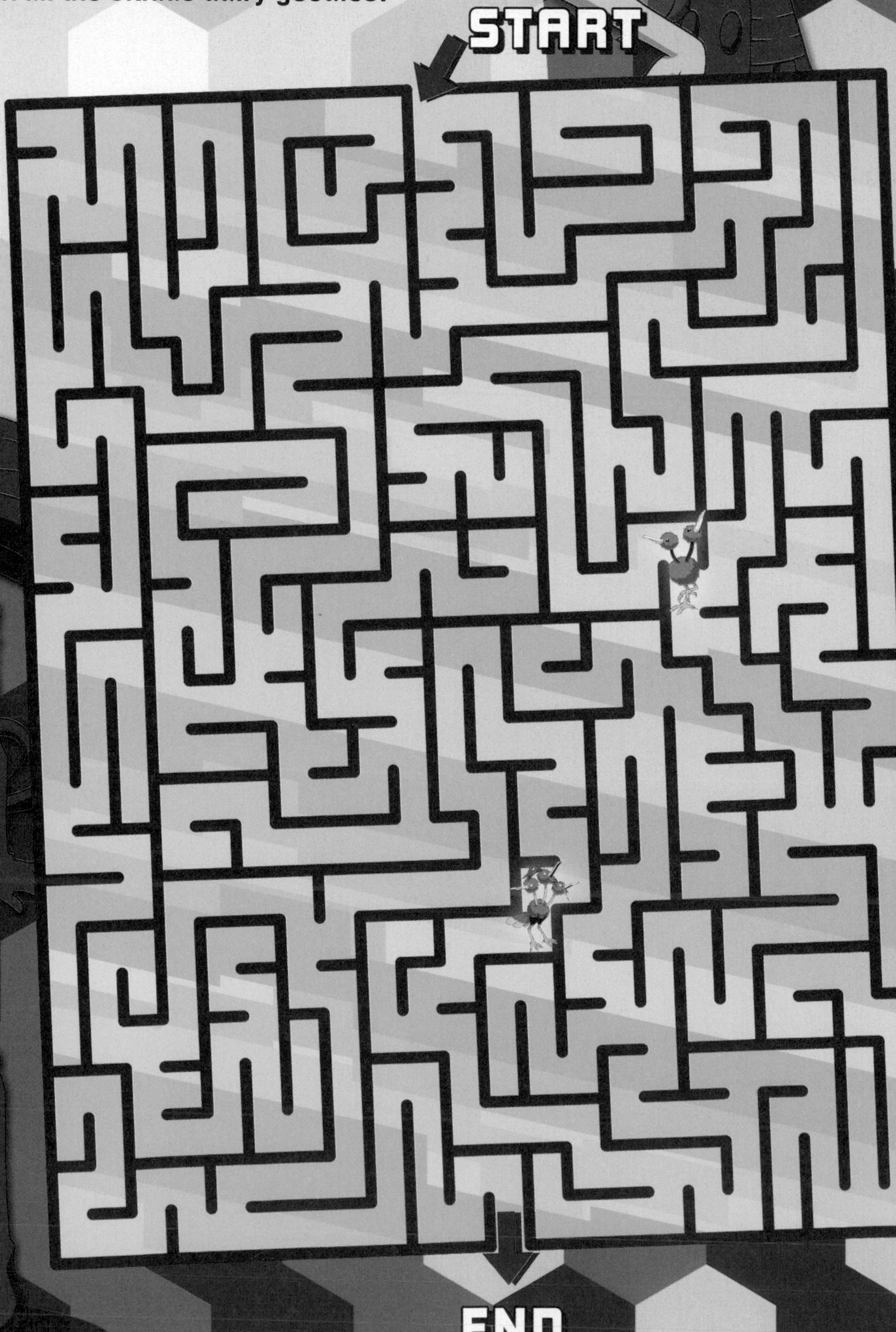

START

END

SKIDDO
COPY COLOUR

Calm and gentle, the Skiddo have been living side by side with people for many generations. They can create energy via photosynthesis. When you hold their horns while riding them, they can sense your feelings.

Copy this soft-natured Pokémon into the grid below. It might give you a ride around the ranch afterwards!

SKIDDO
Mount Pokémon

REGION: Kalos Central subregion

TYPE: Grass

HEIGHT: 0.9m

WEIGHT: 31.0kg

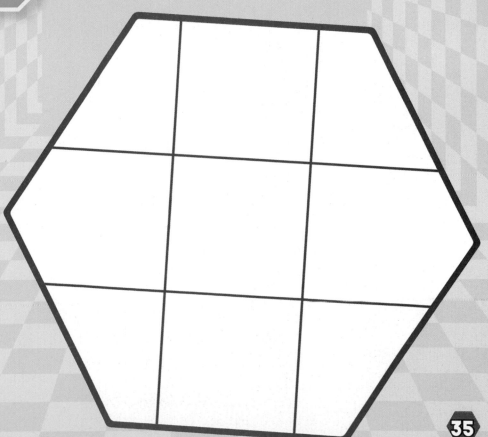

STORY: A STEALTHY CHALLENGE

As Ash and his friends travel to Courmarine City, their journey takes an unexpected diversion when they run into an old friend floating down a river with his Pokémon, Greninja, both unconscious...

"Guys... look! What's that floating down the river?" asked Bonnie.
"Oh no! It's my ninja friend, Sanpei," cried Ash. "Quick, grab him."
Clemont and Ash heaved Sanpei and his Pokémon onto the banks of the river.
"Sanpei, wake up, please wake up!" called Ash.

"Ash? What are you doing here and where is Greninja?" cried Sanpei in a panic, as he slowly came around.
"Don't worry, Greninja's here," said Clemont. "I've given it a Pecha Berry to cure its poisoning. It should feel better in no time."
"Thank you all, you've saved us. I'm so grateful!" sighed Sanpei.
"No problem. But what happened to you guys?" asked Serena.
"Well..." started Sanpei, when out of the bushes jumped a masked ninja.
"There you are!" shouted the ninja.
"Barbaracle, Water Spout!"
"Hey, what's going on?" cried Ash.
"They're the two that attacked us earlier," explained Sanpei.
"Very soon the secret scroll will be mine!" cried the masked ninja as he and his Pokémon launched another attack.

Ash's Froakie and Pikachu leapt into the battle to help defend Sanpei and Greninja.

Unbeknown to the battling friends, yet another problem was lurking in the bushes near by... Team Rocket!
"Well, this is fun!" laughed James. "I never thought I'd witness a ninja Pokémon battle all the way out here in the wild."
"This is our chance to catch Pikachu, whilst those twerps are preoccupied!" giggled Jessie.

"Sanpei, Ash, quick, we need to get out of here," shouted Clemont.
Under the cover of a Ninja Leaf Shroud, the friends quickly disappeared into the forest.

"Phew! Who was that guy and what did he mean about the secret scroll?" asked Ash.
Sanpei scanned the trees around them, before pulling out an ancient-looking scroll.
"He meant this. My master and trainer sent me on a mission to deliver this scroll before sundown today."
Sanpei explained that the scroll contained ninja techniques, passed down for generations in his village, and that he had to deliver it to their fellow ninja comrades who lived in a manor on the other side of the mountain.
"It's getting late. I'd better be on my way," continued Sanpei.
"We'll come with you. We can't let you face these dangers on your own," said Ash.

Meanwhile...
"Where did those twerps disappear to?" cried Jessie. "They've got to be around here somewhere," moaned Meowth. "Look! Footprints. Let's follow them..." said James.

Back on the mountain path...
"Sanpei, if you're going to deliver this scroll before sundown, we're going to have to take the shortcut you mentioned," said Ash.
"But it's dangerous, and I don't want to put you guys at risk," sighed Sanpei.
"We can do it!" cried Bonnie. "Right, Clemont, we can, can't we?"

Clemont looked at the sheer drop down the side of the mountain from the narrow, cracked path they were walking on. "... Sure, er, yes, let's go!" he said, wiping beads of sweat off his forehead.

Suddenly the rocks beneath Clemont's feet started to crumble away! He was falling, flying through the air with Serena next to him. "Arrgghh! Help!" they screamed. "Hang on, don't worry, we've got you!" shouted Ash. Greninja had caught Serena with his super long tongue and Froakie had made a bubble rope to catch Clemont. "Woah! That was close!" whispered Serena, shaking, as she and Clemont were hauled back up the mountain.
"Yeah! I love mountain walks!" groaned Clemont.

"Hey guys! Look!" cried Sanpei.
"No more climbing up the mountain.
There's a cave and it goes down
through the mountain to the other side."
"Awesome, let's go!" cried Ash.
The friends entered the dark cave.

They hadn't been walking for long
when they heard a strange noise.
"What's that sound?" whispered Bonnie.
"A group of Golbat," said Sanpei. "And
they don't like us being in their territory."
"Oh, what are they going to do?"
cried Bonnie.
"Let's not wait around to find out!"
shouted Sanpei. "Greninja, Smokescreen!
Quick, let's go!"
In the confusion and the smoke, Ash
and Sanpei lost the others.
"They must have reached the manor
ahead of us," said Sanpei. "Come
on Ash…"

"Hand over the scroll!" cried
the masked ninja.
"Woah! Where did he come
from?" asked Ash. "We're not
handing anything over!"
"Ash, leave this to me. Go and
find the others," said Sanpei.
"No, I'm not leaving you alone," replied
Ash. "We can win this battle if we work
as a team. Froakie, Pikachu, get
ready to battle!"
Ash and Sanpei fought a fierce
battle with the masked ninja and his
Pokémon, Barbaracle.

Just as they were gaining an upper hand, some other people crept out of the trees.

"Ash, watch out! More enemies over there," cried Sanpei.

"What... oh no, Team Rocket! What do you want?" shouted Ash.

"We've come to catch Pikachu!" grinned Meowth.

"No way!" shouted Ash.

"Stay out of this!" cried the masked Ninja, turning to face the troublesome trio.

"Ahhh, no, they're too powerful! We're blasting off again!" shrieked Jessie. With Team Rocket dispatched, the masked ninja turned back to Ash and Sanpei.

"Let's pick up where we left off!" he cried.

Another fierce battle ensued.

Just as Ash thought they were about to be defeated, something strange happened. There was a burning bright light and then...

"Froakie? Oh wow, you've evolved. You're a Frogadier now. Awesome!" laughed Ash with pride and joy. "Show them your new moves!"

After a lightning flurry of Frogadier's new moves, the masked ninja stepped back.

"OK, we give up," he said.

"What...?" muttered Ash.

"Go to the manor to find your friends," the masked ninja said, mysteriously disappearing into thin air.

Ash and Sanpei set off. They didn't know if they were walking straight into a trap, but they had to get to the manor before sundown.

At last they reached their destination, where a surprise was waiting for them.
"Welcome!" said Clemont.
"Huh? Hey, you guys, how did you get here so quickly?" asked Ash.
"And Master Saizo! What are you doing here? What's going on?" queried Sanpei.
"I'm most impressed you made it all the way here, well done Sanpei," smiled Saizo. "You passed the test with flying colours!"
"Test?" asked Sanpei.
"Yes Sanpei," said Saizo. "You are a ninja who went on a training journey, so I thought I should set you a test to see how much you've grown."

Saizo went on to explain that he was the masked ninja who kept ambushing Sanpei, to test his strength of character and ninja skills.

He had taken the others on ahead to the manor, to keep them out of harm's way. And the secret scroll was actually blank!
"Well, Master, whether the scroll is blank or not, I've delivered it on time, which means my mission is now complete!" laughed Sanpei.
"Indeed. You made a heartfelt connection with your friends, and overcame formidable obstacles with Greninja. You are a truly worthy ninja," said Saizo.
"Hey, Sanpei," laughed Ash. "Now your mission is over, how about a battle? And this time I'll win! Frogadier, are you ready…?

With everyone safely reunited, and another exciting Pokémon adventure over, Ash and his friends set off once again on their journey through Kalos. Next stop, Coumarine City…

Pokémon Battle Moves!

Every Pokémon has its own battle Moves specific to its type or species. Trainers can teach their Pokémon new Moves; perhaps Ash should borrow some from Greninja – a few stealthy ninja Moves would come in handy in a forest ambush!

BARBARACLE
Collective Pokémon

REGION: Kalos Central

TYPE: Rock-Water

HEIGHT: 1.3m

WEIGHT: 96.0kg

When seven Binacle come together to fight as one, a Barbaracle is formed. The head gives the orders, but the limbs don't always listen.

GOLBAT
Bat Pokémon

REGION: Kalos Central

TYPE: Poison-Flying

HEIGHT: 1.6m

WEIGHT: 55.0kg

Golbat feeds on energy from living beings, biting with its huge mouth and sharp fangs. It won't stop until its victim is drained, even if it becomes so full that it can't fly.

GRENINJA
Ninja Pokémon

REGION: Kalos Central

TYPE: Water-Dark

HEIGHT: 1.5m

WEIGHT: 40.0kg

Greninja is the evolved form of Frogadier. It can compress water into sharp-edged throwing stars. With the grace of a ninja, it slips in and out of sight to attack from the shadows.

FROGADIER
Bubble Frog Pokémon

REGION: Kalos Central

TYPE: Water

HEIGHT: 0.6m

WEIGHT: 10.9kg

Swift and sure, Frogadier coats pebbles in a bubbly foam and then flings them with pinpoint accuracy. It has spectacular jumping and climbing skills.

Sanpei's Ninja Mission

Sanpei, Ash's ninja friend, has been given an important mission by his ninja Master, Saizo.
He's got to deliver a secret scroll to a manor house before sundown. Using the Pokémon key, help Sanpei move stealthily through the forest before he gets ambushed again.

DOWN   **UP**   **LEFT**   **RIGHT**

START

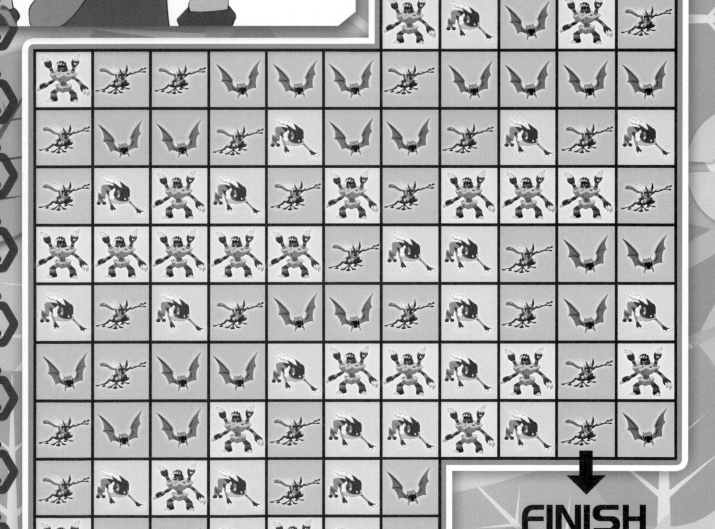

FINISH

NINJA CODEBREAKER

What is the secret to becoming a great ninja? The skills required are pretty similar to those needed to turn a Pokémon Trainer into a Master!

Sanpei has a secret scroll, given to him by his Master, which talks about ancient ninja techniques. He wants to share this information with Ash to help him on his own path to becoming a Pokémon Master, but the scroll is written in code.

Use the Pokémon alphabet code below to help Ash decipher the scroll and the ways of the ninja!

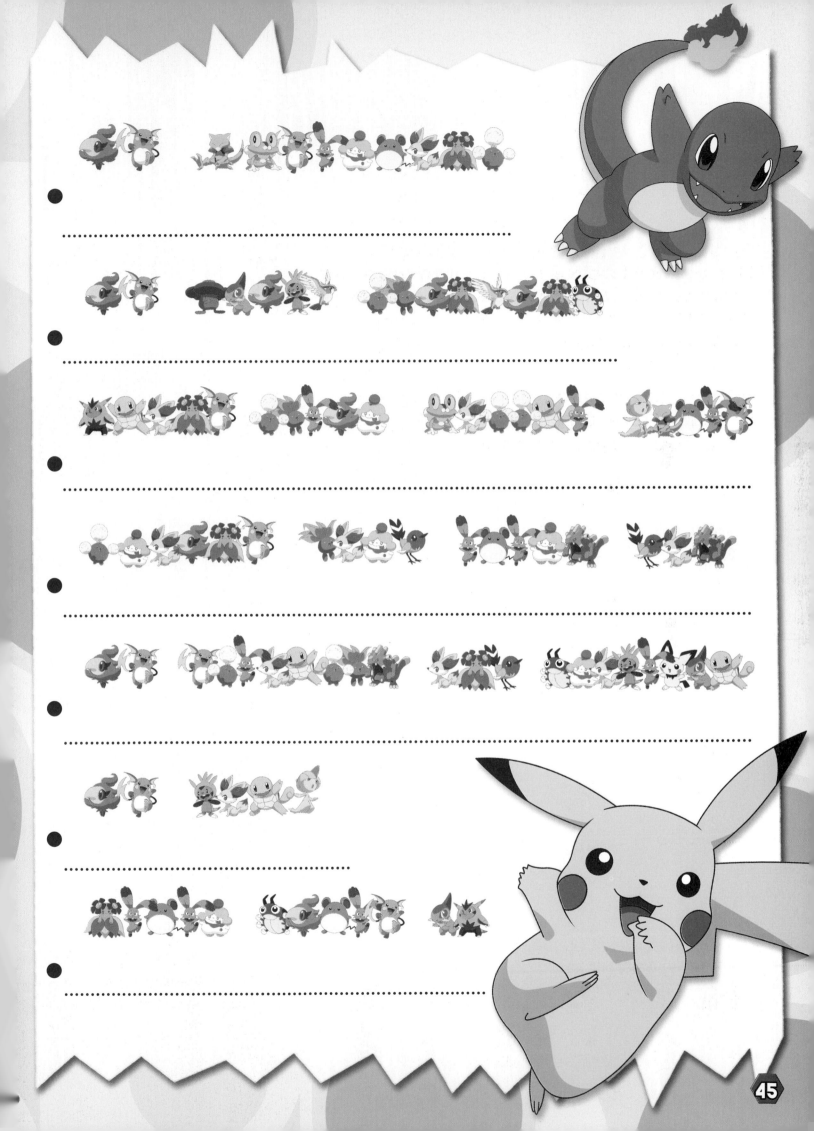

KALOS POKÉMON WHO'S WHO?

Ash and his pals have met a varied mix of new Pokémon species and types on their travels through the ever-changing landscape of Kalos. Help the friends identify these awesome creatures without looking them up on your Pokédex! What a skilled Pokémon Trainer you are!

1

This creature is formed when 7 Binacle come together to fight as one.

....

2

Stories say that this nocturnal Ghost-Grass type Pokémon serves as a guide for wandering spirits!

....

3

The milk from this gentle creature makes delicious ice cream and cheese.

....

4

This Fairy-type Pokémon uses its flower as an energy source.

....

5

This Plump Mouse Pokémon gnaws on rock or wood to keep its front teeth worn down.

....

6

Don't touch this Dragon Pokémon! Its body is covered in bristling spikes.

....

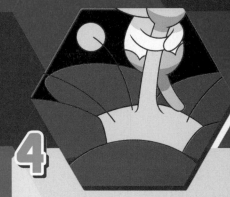

7

This Caring Pokémon is certainly true to its nature. It helps heal injured Pokémon!

....

POKÉMON TYPE TEST

Push yourself to your limits by matching each of these Pokémon to their correct type or dual type.

1. Pikachu
2. Golbat
3. Starmie
4. Meowth
5. Ledyba
6. Wobbuffet
7. Pancham
8. Fletchinder
9. Chespin
10. Dedenne

GRASS

NORMAL

ELECTRIC

POISON-FLYING

ELECTRIC-FAIRY

PSYCHIC

WATER-PSYCHIC

BUG-FLYING

FIGHTING

FIRE-FLYING

POKÉMON EVOLUTION – MISSING LINKS

The missing Pokémon are pictured at the bottom of the page to give you a helping hand.

Every Pokémon Trainer needs to keep up-to-date with Pokémon Evolution. Ash and his friends have learned a lot about this special subject from Professor Sycamore, a prominent Pokémon researcher based in Kalos. He is at the forefront of groundbreaking research on Pokémon Evolution.

Test out your own Pokémon Evolution knowledge by filling in the missing Pokémon in each Evolution chain. Ash got them all correct, so no pressure!

1 .... — Pikachu — ....

2 Froakie — .... — ....

3 .... —  Quilladin — ....

4 .... — .... — Delphox

5 Shinx — .... — Luxray

6 .... —  Grovyle — Sceptile

7 .... —  Marshtomp — Swampert

8  Torchic — Combusken — ....

 Blaziken

 Braixen

 Luxio

 Raichu

 Chesnaught

Mudkip Fennekin Pichu Treecko Frogadier Greninja Chespin

48

EEVEE, THE EVOLUTION POKÉMON

The amazingly adaptive Eevee can evolve into many different Pokémon depending on its environment. This allows it to withstand harsh conditions. It is a Normal Type Pokémon from the Kanto region.

How well do you know your Eevee Evolutions? Name all the different Eevee evolved Pokémon. Look at the images and stats to help you. So far, there is only one Kalos Eevee Evolution Pokémon. It belongs to the new Fairy Type Pokémon group. Who is it?

1

NAME: **EEVEE**
....
Evolution Pokémon
TYPE: Normal
REGION: Kanto / Kalos

2

NAME: ....
Intertwining Pokémon
TYPE: Fairy
REGION: Kanto / Kalos

3

NAME: ....
Lightning Pokémon
TYPE: Electric
REGION: Kanto / Kalos

4

NAME: ....
Bubble Jet Pokémon
TYPE: Water
REGION: Kanto / Kalos

5

NAME: ....
Flame Pokémon
TYPE: Fire
REGION: Kanto / Kalos

6

NAME: ....
Sun Pokémon
TYPE: Psychic
REGION: Johto/ Kalos

7

NAME: ....
Moonlight Pokémon
TYPE: Dark
REGION: Johto / Kalos

8

NAME: ....
Fresh Snow Pokémon
TYPE: Ice
REGION: Sinnoh / Kalos

9

NAME: ....
Verdant Pokémon
TYPE: Grass
REGION: Sinnoh / Kalos

STORY: FACING THE GRAND DESIGN

During their journey to Coumarine City, Ash and his friends come across a Malamar in the forest at the foot of a strange craggy mountain called Grace Tower. Team Rocket is also in the same forest — on a Pikachu hunt as usual — but when they come across another Malamar, Inkay starts acting out of character...

"Hey, isn't that a Malamar guys?" asked Serena.
"Yes it is," replied Clemont. "Be careful, don't look at its light. Remember that bad Malamar who hypnotised us that time..."

Suddenly the Malamar disappeared into the trees. The friends followed it, until they came to a road at the edge of a forest clearing. To their surprise they saw lots of Malamar, Inkay, Flabébé, Bidoof and Ledyba feeding happily together on berries.
"Oh, how cute, they look like they're all good friends," giggled Bonnie.
"I guess the Malamar that live here are really nice..." said Ash. "...Hey, watch out!"
Ash and his friends had to launch themselves out of the way as three huge lorries raced past them on their way up the rocky mountain, nearly running them over.

"What are they doing? Someone needs to teach them to drive!" shouted Ash.
"They're going up that strange-looking mountain," said Serena.
"That's where the UFOs and aliens live!" giggled Bonnie.
"I already told you, there's no scientific proof that they exist…" started Clemont.
"Well, I say let's climb up there and see for ourselves!" laughed Ash.
"Really? You want to climb up there?" muttered Clemont.
"Come on guys, it'll be fun!" said Ash.

Meanwhile…
Team Rocket had seen the lorries too, as they climbed up the mountain after Inkay, who was still acting strangely. When three huge diamond-like structures floated out of the lorries, followed by three evil-looking Malamar, Inkay flew into a wild rage.

"Oh no!" cried James. "They're the wicked Malamar from the radio observatory that were trying to take over the world."
"I wouldn't be surprised if Inkay sent them after us. Don't forget Inkay evolves into Malamar," screeched Meowth. "I bet they're all in cahoots!"
"Run!" screamed Jessie, as the three evil creatures spotted them.

"Team Rocket!" said Serena, as the trio came tearing down the mountain road and bundled into the group of friends.
"What are you doing here?"
"We haven't got time to explain. We've got big problems, and so will you if you don't hide right now!" screeched Jessie.
"What's going on…?" said Ash.
"Pssst! Quick, all of you, in here, now!" cried a voice from the shadows.

Everyone turned towards the voice. It was coming out of a dark cave entrance.
"Hurry!" the voice said urgently. Everyone ran into the cave, just as the three Malamar flew past.
"Oh, that was too close!" Clemont shivered.
"I'll explain everything later, Ash," said the voice.
"Hold on, how do you know my name?" asked Ash.
"I know Team Rocket is your enemy, but for now we need a truce," the voice continued, as the person owning it took off their hat.
"Officer Jenny!" cried Bonnie.
"Oh it's so good to see you again."

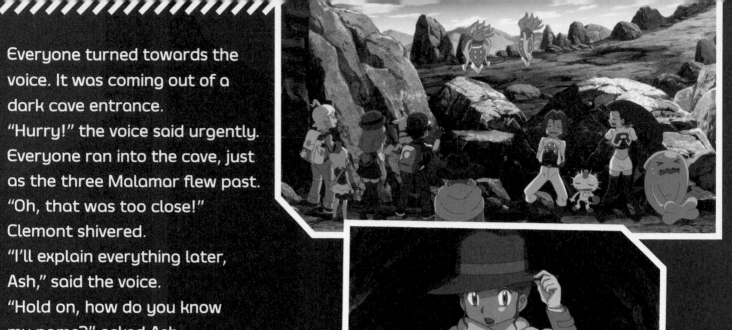

"What's going on?" asked Clemont.
"Well, it's a long story…"
Officer Jenny told everyone about her secret investigation into the evil Malamar that were trying to take over the world. They had manipulated the Kalos region's most distinguished scientists into activating a scientific device for use as a weapon. This device was now sitting at the top of Grace Tower Mountain. The Malamar were plotting to use it somehow in their grand design to control the world.
"But don't worry kids. I will stop them no matter what their plan may be," finished Officer Jenny.
"Er, Officer Jenny, it may be too late… the Malamar are outside!" cried Serena.
Everyone ran out of the cave to see what was going on.

"What is that ball of light? Arrgh…!" screamed Jessie, as she floated up into the air, trapped by a ray of light. The same thing then happened to Ash, Bonnie, Serena and Officer Jenny.

"What are we going to do now?" cried Serena.
"Don't worry guys," shouted Clemont. "We'll find a way to rescue you. Quick, James, Meowth, Inkay, follow me."
"We're counting on you!" shouted Ash. Before the light could trap them too, Clemont, James, Meowth and Inkay tunnelled out of the cave, using Clemont's Bunnelby to dig the way out for them.

Back in the forest, Inkay became really angry.
"It's mad because those evil Malamar were trying to control you James," translated Meowth, as Inkay gibbered away. "It's going to knock their blocks off!"
"Go Inkay! But we need a plan. Those Malamar are really strong. We don't stand a chance against them by ourselves," said Clemont. Suddenly, Inkay dashed off into the forest.
"I bet it's got an idea. Let's follow it!" cried James.
"Inkay's asking the forest Malamar to help us fight the evil Malamar!" said Meowth. "They're upset because the evil Malamar attacked their buddies, and they're going to join us!"

Back on the mountain, the evil Malamar had started the countdown to activating their grand plan. The huge diamond structures were glowing red.
"Where is Clemont?" cried Bonnie. "I don't want the world to end like this. I'm scared!"
"Oh here they are, at last!" sighed Serena.
"Sorry guys, it took a bit of time to rally some support," said James.
The mountainside path was filling up with all the good Malamar and Inkay from the forest.
"Let's finish this off!" cried Meowth.

"Inkay, no old chum!" screamed James. "What are you doing? You're meant to be on our side."
"He's being hypnotised by that evil Malamar to join forces with them!" translated Meowth.
"Please, Inkay. Don't let our bond be severed by that creep!" shouted James, holding out a croissant, Inkay's favourite food. "Remember our days together. We're partners!"
Inkay snapped out of its trance and flew into James' arms.
"He's back!" cheered James. "Ok, Inkay, it's payback time! So use Tackle and let's seal the deal!"
One of the evil Malamar fell to the ground.
"Pikachu, let's get in there too," shouted Ash. "Thunderbolt!"
A fierce battle began.

Suddenly the ball of light started disappearing and the red light on the floating diamond structures started fading away.

"It's over!" said Officer Jenny to the evil Malamar. "Your plan has failed. Now come with me quietly."

But the evil Malamar rushed away, chanting their evil words.

"They're escaping into the future," translated Meowth. "But they'll be back to fight again. And when they return, their grand design will finally succeed."

The friends rushed down the mountain path, as rocks started falling and explosions could be heard all around them.

"What are they doing?" asked Serena.

"They're destroying all the evidence of their scheme," said Clemont.

"Well, at least we stopped them this time!" said Ash.

An unlikely group of long-time foes joined forces to stop the evil Malamar from taking over the world and putting their terrifying plans in place. The day was a triumph!

But now, Ash and his friends must carry on with their journey through Kalos to Coumarine and Ash's next Gym battle. And as for the terrible trio, Team Rocket, sadly one good deed is not going to change their criminal ways, when there is still an elusive Pikachu to catch! The adventures continue...

FOREST CREATURES

Ash and his friends discover more Pokémon in the forest at the foot of the strange Grace Tower Mountain. Check out the stats for these interesting forest creatures. Just watch out for the Malamar – they can mess with your mind!

MALAMAR
Overturning Pokémon

REGION: Kalos Coastal

TYPE: Dark-Psychic

HEIGHT: 1.5m

WEIGHT: 47.0kg

With hypnotic compulsion, Malamar can control the actions of others, forcing them to do things at its will. The movement of its tentacles can put anyone watching into a trance.

FLABÉBÉ
Single Bloom Pokémon

REGION: Kalos Central

TYPE: Fairy

HEIGHT: 0.1m

WEIGHT: 0.1kg

Each Flabébé has a special connection with the flower it holds. They take care of their flowers and use them as an energy source.

BIDOOF
Plump Mouse Pokémon

REGION: Kalos Central

TYPE: Normal

HEIGHT: 0.5m

WEIGHT: 20.0kg

Bidoof live beside the water, where they gnaw on rock or wood to keep their front teeth worn down. They have a steady nature and are not easily upset.

LEDYBA
Five Star Pokémon

REGION: Kalos Central

TYPE: Bug-Flying

HEIGHT: 1.0m

WEIGHT: 10.8kg

In cold weather, many Ledyba swarm to the same place, forming a big cluster to keep each other warm. These timid Pokémon also tend to stick together for protection.

MANECTRIC
Discharge Pokémon

REGION: Kalos Coastal

TYPE: Electric

HEIGHT: 1.5m

WEIGHT: 40.2kg

In places where lightning strikes the ground, Manectric makes its nest. Its mane gives off an electric charge.

KALOS QUIZ!

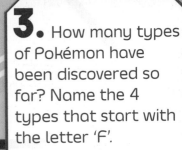

Are you up for the challenge? Test your Kalos Pokémon knowledge by answering these 10 questions as quickly as you can.

1. In which city does Ash's fourth Gym Battle challenge take place?

....

2. What is the name of Ash's ninja warrior friend?

....

3. How many types of Pokémon have been discovered so far? Name the 4 types that start with the letter 'F'.

....

....

....

....

4. What is the name of the Kalos mythical Pokémon?

....

5. Name the 6 regions Ash has travelled through so far.

....

....

....

....

....

6. What job do Eddy and Lindsey do?

....

7. The milk from which Pokémon makes delicious ranch ice cream and cheese?

....

8. Which Pokémon evolves from a Frogadier?

....

9. Ash and his friends meet a Malamar at the foot of which Kalos mountain?

....

10. Name the first Pokémon that Jessie catches in Kalos.

....

SCORE:
/10

....

57

TWENTY YEARS ON...

Ash Ketchum and his loyal buddy, Pikachu, have had many awesome adventures over the years and met lots of new friends and, of course, hundreds of new Pokémon! Their journey on the path towards Ash becoming a Pokémon Master started back in Pallet Town in the Kanto region.

JOHTO

Geography: Similar terrain to Kanto, but more rural. Temperate climate, but wetter than Kanto.

First Partner Pokémon: Chikorita (Grass), Cyndaquil (Fire), Totodile (Water)

Legendary Pokémon: Raikou, Entei, Suicune, Lugia, Ho-Oh

Mythical Pokémon: Celebi

Ash's travelling companions: (No new companions) Misty, Brock

KANTO

Geography: Mainly forests and plains with several mountain ranges. Temperate climate.

First Partner Pokémon: Squirtle (Water), Charmander (Fire), Bulbasaur (Grass-Poison)

Legendary Pokémon: Articuno, Zapdos, Moltres, Mewtwo

Mythical Pokémon: Mew

Ash's travelling companions: Misty, Brock

Since then, the inseparable pair has travelled through the incredible regions of Johto, Hoenn, Sinnoh and Unova. Currently, their journey is taking them through the vast and varied landscapes of the Kalos region.

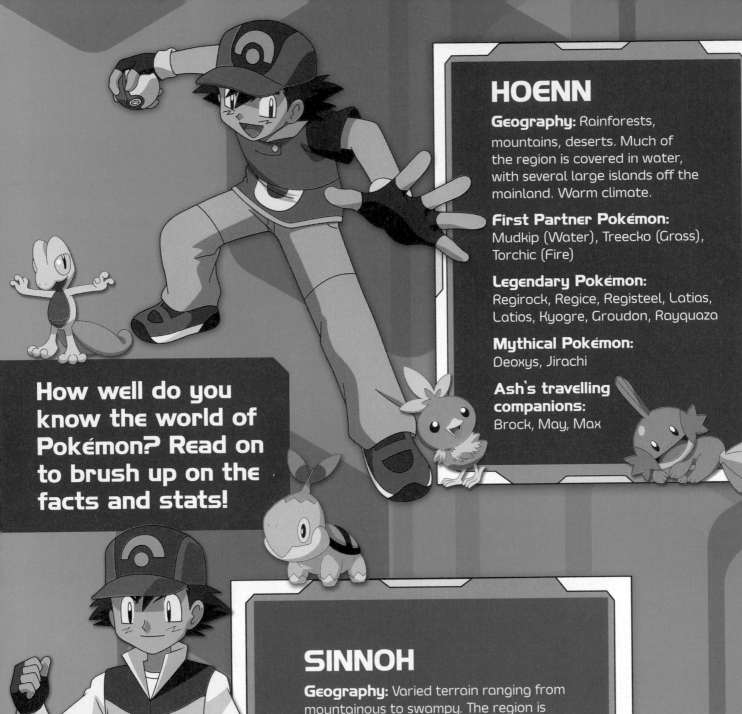

How well do you know the world of Pokémon? Read on to brush up on the facts and stats!

HOENN

Geography: Rainforests, mountains, deserts. Much of the region is covered in water, with several large islands off the mainland. Warm climate.

First Partner Pokémon: Mudkip (Water), Treecko (Grass), Torchic (Fire)

Legendary Pokémon: Regirock, Regice, Registeel, Latias, Latios, Kyogre, Groudon, Rayquaza

Mythical Pokémon: Deoxys, Jirachi

Ash's travelling companions: Brock, May, Max

SINNOH

Geography: Varied terrain ranging from mountainous to swampy. The region is rich in water (4 large lakes). The climate is generally colder than the other regions, with snow in the northern parts.

First Partner Pokémon: Piplup (Water), Chimchar (Fire), Turtwig (Grass)

Legendary Pokémon: Uxie, Mesprit, Azelf, Dialga, Palkia, Heatran, Regiggas, Giratina, Cresselia

Mythical Pokémon: Manaphy, Darkrai, Shaymin, Arceus, Phione

Ash's travelling companions: Brock, Dawn

UNOVA

Geography: Urban and rural region, divided into three landmasses by two rivers. Includes several forests, a desert and some mountain ranges. Climate is seasonal, unlike any of the other regions.

First Partner Pokémon: Snivy (Grass), Tepig (Fire), Oshawott (Water)

Legendary Pokémon: Cobalion, Terrakion, Virizion, Tornadus, Thundurus, Landorus, Zekrom, Reshiram, Kyurem, Black Kyurem, White Kyurem

Mythical Pokémon: Victini, Keldeo, Meloetta, Genesect

Ash's travelling companions: Iris, Cilan

KALOS

Geography: Vast, varied landscape including rivers, mountains, forest, caves, rocky coastal cliffs, beaches and marshlands. Divided into three distinct subregions — Central, Coastal and Mountain. Temperate climate; cooler and some snow in the mountains.

First Partner Pokémon: Fennekin (Fire), Froakie (Water), Chespin (Grass)

Legendary Pokémon: Xerneas, Yveltal, Zygarde

Mythical Pokémon: Diancie, Hoopa

Ash's travelling companions: Clemont, Bonnie, Serena

ANSWERS

PAGE 14

PAGE 30

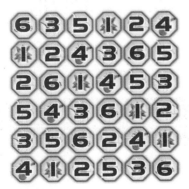

REMORAID
QWILFISH
SKRELP
DRAGALGE
LUVDISC
HUNTAIL
MURAILLE
SSLER
CHINCHOU
MAGIKARP

PAGE 31

6 3 5 1 2 4
1 2 4 3 6 5
2 6 1 4 5 3
5 4 3 6 1 2
3 5 6 2 4 1
4 1 2 5 3 6

The 6 Pokémon are:
1. Starmie
2. Chinchou
3. Magikarp
4. Seadra
5. Remoraid
6. Octillery

PAGE 34

PAGE 43

PAGE 44

- is observant
- is quick-thinking
- plans their battle moves
- trains hard every day
- is stealthy and graceful
- is calm
- never gives up

PAGE 46

1. Barbaracle
2. Pumpkaboo
3. Skiddo
4. Flabébé
5. Bidoof
6. Seadra
7. Alomomola

PAGE 47

1. Pikachu — ELECTRIC
2. Golbat — POISON-FLYING
3. Starmie — WATER-PSYCHIC
4. Meowth — NORMAL
5. Ledyba — BUG-FLYING
6. Wobbuffet — PSYCHIC
7. Pancham — FIGHTING
8. Fletchinder — FIRE-FLYING
9. Chespin — GRASS
10. Dedenne — ELECTRIC-FAIRY

PAGE 48

1. Pichu – Pikachu – Raichu
2. Froakie – Frogadier – Greninja
3. Chespin – Quilladin – Chesnaught
4. Fennekin – Braixen – Delphox
5. Shinx – Luxio – Luxray
6. Treecko – Grovyle – Sceptile
7. Mudkip – Marshtomp – Swampert
8. Torchic – Combusken – Blaziken

PAGE 49

1. Eevee
2. Sylveon
   (the only Kalos Eevee Evolution so far).
3. Jolteon
4. Vaporeon
5. Flareon
6. Espeon
7. Umbreon
8. Glaceon
9. Leafeon

PAGE 57

1. Coumarine, Kalos
2. Sanpei
3. There are 18 types of Pokémon. The 4 types that start with the letter 'F' are: Fire, Flying, Fighting and Fairy.
4. Diancie
5. Kanto, Johto, Hoenn, Sinnoh, Unova, Kalos
6. They are underwater archeologists
7. The milk from the Skiddo
8. Greninja
9. Grace Tower
10. Pumpkaboo